IOWA
ASSESSMENTS™
GRADE 3
PRACTICE TEST

Pascal Prep™

Please leave a review for this book!

Thank you for purchasing this resource.

Please leave a review on the website where you purchased this publication.

TABLE OF CONTENTS

INTRODUCTION

About Iowa Assessments™..4

How To Use This Book..5

Test-Taking Tips..5

PRACTICE TEST

Reading..6

Written Expression..18

Mathematics...29

Vocabulary...45

Spelling..49

Capitalization...53

Punctuation..57

Computation (Mathematics)...61

Word Analysis..66

Listening..70

Science...76

Social Studies...82

QUESTION TEXTS & ANSWER KEYS

Word Analysis Question Text...89

Listening Question Text...90

Answer Key..94

About Iowa Assessments™

- Iowa Assessments™ measure a student's skills in reading, language, math, social studies, and science.
- The assessment identifies strengths and challenges at the individual student level, as well as for the overall class/grade level.
- Schools use the results to evaluate student/class performance.
- In some cases, schools use the results for gifted/advanced program placement.

Iowa Assessments™ Structure & Administration

- The assessment is timed. The core test lasts around four hours. The full test, including optional sections, lasts around six hours.
- The test is given in a group setting.
- Check with your school to see which sections they plan to administer.
- Some schools do not administer the optional sections, including Word Analysis, Listening, Social Studies, and Science.
- Before the test starts, a test administrator reads the questions aloud. Then, students will read the test questions on their own.
- Students are allowed to go back to questions, should they want to change an answer - as long as the questions are in the same section.
- Students can use scratch paper for working out math problems, for example.

Test Section: Number of Questions / Number of Minutes

Test Section	Questions / Minutes	Test Section	Questions / Minutes
Reading:	41 / 60 mins	Written Expression:	35 / 40 mins
Mathematics:	50 / 60 mins	Vocabulary:	29 / 15 mins
Spelling:	24 / 10 mins	Capitalization:	20 / 10 mins
Punctuation:	20 / 10 mins	Computation:	25 / 20 mins
Word Analysis:	33 / 20 mins	Listening:	28 / 25 mins
Social Studies:	30 / 35 mins	Science:	30 / 35 mins

Iowa Assessments™ Scoring

- Student scores and performance are presented in an Individual Profile Narrative.
- This score report includes a national percentile rank (NPR), percentile ranges, highlights strengths and weaknesses, tracks progress (if the student has taken the test before), and explains the scores for parents, teachers, and school administrators.
- The report includes data on test performance overall and in the individual subject areas. (Note that this practice test cannot produce an accurate score because it has not been given to a large enough group of students to yield an accurate comparison / calculation.)

How To Use This Book

1. Cut out pages 89-98.

- Pages 89-93 contain the questions you must read to your child for Word Analysis & Listening.

- Pages 94-98 contain the Answer Key for the Practice Test.

2. Do one or two sections per day (if time allows).

- The test sections begin on page 6 with the Reading section.

- Like the real test, this book has 12 sections.

3. Before beginning each section, read through the section's brief intro material. Then, do the example(s) together with your child. This ensures they know what to expect from the questions.

4. Depending on your child's abilities, you may allow them to do the rest of the section on their own.

- Check in to see how they are progressing, using the answer key.

- If they need help, step in so they do not complete an entire section incorrectly.

5. After finishing the practice test, go through and check your child's answers.

- This will give you an idea of your child's strengths/challenges, pertaining to each test section.

- For questions missed, go over the answers again, discussing what makes the correct answer better than the other choices.

Test-Taking Tips

- No points are deducted for wrong answers. So, it is best for your child to at least guess.
- Use process of elimination. (Get rid of any answers that are clearly not correct, then guess from those remaining.)
- Make sure they do not rush through questions. (There is no prize for finishing first!)
- If a question is too hard, move to the next one and return to it if time allows at the end. (You are allowed to go back to a question if it is in the same section that you are working on.)
- Do not get stressed about the test! There will be some questions where you may not know the answer. Instead of getting stressed, just focus on doing your best.
- This tip/suggestion is entirely at parent's discretion. Parents may wish to offer some sort of special motivation to encourage a child to do their best. An extra incentive of, for example, an art set, a building brick set, or a special outing can go a long way in motivating young learners!
- The night before testing, it is imperative that children have enough sleep, without any interruptions. (Think about the difference in your brain function with a good night's sleep vs. without. The same goes for your child's brain function.)
- The morning before the test, ensure your child eats a healthy breakfast with protein and complex carbs. Do not let them eat sugar, chocolate, etc.

Reading

- The Reading section consists of 8 passages, followed by a set of questions.

- After reading each passage, students answer a set of questions on passage content.

- Be sure that your child carefully reads the passage and each part of the question.

- Be sure that they understand what the question is asking.

- An arrow (⬅) means there will be a question about a word on this line. Use context clues in the sentence or passage to figure out the word's meaning.

- Students have 60 minutes to complete this section.

- Below is an example passage and question.

Example Passage

Honeybees play a <u>crucial</u> role in pollinating flowers, helping plants grow, and producing food. A single honeybee can visit hundreds of flowers in one day, collecting nectar to bring back to the hive. Inside the hive, bees work together to turn the nectar into honey, which they store for food. Honeybees live in highly organized colonies with a queen bee, worker bees, and drones. Each of these has a specific role to ensure the hive runs smoothly.

Question for the Example Passage

Find the word "<u>crucial</u>" in the passage. In the passage, the word "crucial" is closest in meaning to which of the choices below?

A. light
B. second
C. very important
D. possible

The answer is C. (Crucial is closest in meaning to "very important.")

Reading Passage 1

Lions are known as the "king of the jungle," but they actually live in grasslands and savannas, not jungles. These large cats are social animals that live in groups called prides. A pride typically consists of several female lions, their cubs, and a few male lions. Female lions do most of the hunting, working together to take down prey such as zebras and antelope.

Male lions, on the other hand, are responsible for protecting the pride from threats. They use their powerful roars to warn off other animals and to communicate with members of the pride. Lions spend most of their day resting and are usually only active during the early morning or evening when it's cooler.

Despite their strength, lions face many challenges. Habitat loss and illegal hunting are major threats to their survival, and conservation efforts are essential to protect these magnificent creatures.

Questions for Reading Passage 1

1. What is a group of lions called?

A. A pack

B. A herd

C. A pride

D. A colony

2. What is the main job of male lions in a pride?

A. Hunting for food

B. Protecting the pride

C. Raising the cubs

D. Teaching the female lions

3. When are lions most active?

A. In the early morning and evening

B. During the night

C. During the afternoon

D. Throughout the entire day

4. What is one challenge that lions face in the wild?

A. Sandstorms

B. Habitat loss

C. A lack of water

D. Other animals in their pride

Reading Passage 2

Dolphins are known for their intelligence and social behavior. These marine mammals live in groups called pods, which can range from just a few dolphins to over a hundred. Dolphins communicate with each other using a series of clicks, whistles, and body movements. This complex system of communication helps them work together to hunt for food and protect each other from predators.

Dolphins are also known for their playful nature. They can often be seen jumping out of the water, riding waves, and even interacting with humans. In some cases, dolphins have been known to help rescue humans in danger, such as guiding stranded swimmers to safety.

Despite their friendly and intelligent nature, dolphins face many threats. Pollution, fishing nets, and habitat loss are just some of the dangers that dolphins encounter in the wild. Conservation efforts are ongoing to protect these remarkable creatures and ensure their survival.

Questions for Reading Passage 2

1. What is the purpose of dolphins' communication system?

A. To scare away predators   C. To communicate, protect each other, and hunt
B. To play with humans   D. To learn new tricks

2. What is a group of dolphins called?

A. A herd   B. A school   C. A pod   D. A pack

3. What behavior shows that dolphins are playful?

A. They use their communication system.
B. They help rescue humans in danger.
C. They protect each other from predators.
D. They are seen jumping out of the water and riding waves.

4. What are some man-made threats that dolphins face in the wild?

A. Sharks, whales, and stingrays   C. Cold water
B. Pollution, fishing nets, and habitat loss   D. Large storms

Reading Passage 3

Dreams   *a poem by Langston Hughes*

Hold fast to dreams
For if dreams die
Life is a broken-winged bird
That cannot fly.

Hold fast to dreams
For when dreams go
Life is a barren field
Frozen with snow.

Questions for Reading Passage 3

1. What does the speaker suggest will happen if "dreams die"?

A. The reader will wake up from dreaming.
B. Life will go on slowly.
C. Life will feel hopeless.
D. Life will end.

2. What description does the speaker use to explain a life without dreams?

A. A barren field frozen with snow
B. A river flowing slowly
C. A journey across a desert
D. A fallen tree

3. What does the phrase "hold fast to dreams" mean in the context of the poem?

A. Let go of your dreams.
B. Hang onto your dreams tightly.
C. Quickly come up with ideas for your dreams.
D. Have dreams that are easy to understand.

4. How does the imagery of a "broken-winged bird" and a "barren field" relate to the poem's message?

A. They show that dreams should have to do with nature.
B. They describe the narrator's past.
C. They show that it's best to let go of dreams when you are sad.
D. They show the sadness of losing dreams.

Reading Passage 4

In a peaceful village, there lived a young boy named Thomas who dreamed of becoming a master baker. Every day, he would visit the village bakery, watching the baker knead dough and shape loaves of bread. Thomas would spend hours imagining himself making the perfect loaf.

One morning, the baker noticed Thomas peering through the window and invited him inside. "Would you like to help me today?" the baker asked. Thomas eagerly nodded, and the baker handed him an apron. Thomas worked hard, learning how to measure flour, mix ingredients, and shape dough.

Weeks passed, and Thomas became quite skilled. One day, the baker fell ill, and Thomas was asked to bake the bread for the village. Nervously, Thomas agreed. With steady hands, he mixed the ingredients and placed the loaves in the oven. When the bread was ready, the villagers tasted it and smiled. "This is the best bread we've ever had!" they exclaimed. Thomas realized that with practice and patience, his dream of becoming a great baker was coming true.

Questions for Reading Passage 4

1. Why did Thomas visit the village bakery every day?

A. He wanted to learn how to bake.
B. He liked to eat bread.
C. He had to deliver flour.
D. He was working for the baker.

2. How did Thomas learn to bake?

A. By watching the baker through the window
B. By reading cookbooks
C. By his parents teaching him
D. By helping the baker in the bakery

3. Why did the baker ask Thomas to bake the bread one day?

A. The baker had too much work to do.
B. The baker got sick and couldn't bake.
C. The villagers wanted to try the bread Thomas had made.
D. Thomas asked to bake the bread.

4. How did the villagers react to Thomas's bread?

A. They said it was good, but needed to be cooked more.
B. They said it was the best bread they had ever tasted.
C. They didn't notice the difference.
D. They were upset that the baker wasn't there.

5. What did Thomas learn about becoming a great baker?

A. It takes practice and patience.
B. It requires only a little time and preparation.
C. It is impossible without the baker's help.
D. The villagers will always help him.

Reading Passage 5

Many birds migrate long distances every year. One of the most well-known migratory birds is the Arctic tern. These small birds travel from their breeding grounds in the Arctic all the way to Antarctica. This journey can be over 25,000 miles round trip, making them the birds with the longest migration in the world. During their migration, Arctic terns fly over vast stretches of ocean, relying on strong winds and ocean currents to help them along the way. They also use stars and the sun to <u>navigate</u>. ⬅

Unlike some birds that migrate for food, Arctic terns migrate to follow the summer season. This means that they experience more daylight than any other animal on Earth. By flying between the Arctic and Antarctic, they take advantage of the long days of summer in both regions.

Questions for Reading Passage 5

1. Find the word "navigate" in the passage. In the passage, the word "navigate" is closest in meaning to which word?

A. use as light
B. use to guide the way
C. watch
D. hunt

2. How long is the Arctic tern's migration journey?

A. 10,000 miles
B. 15,000 miles
C. 25,000 miles
D. 30,000 miles

3. What helps Arctic terns during their migration?

A. Strong winds and ocean currents
B. The color of their feathers
C. Flying in large groups
D. The position of the planets

4. Why do Arctic terns migrate?

A. To escape rainy weather
B. To find the best spot to lay their eggs
C. To avoid predators
D. To follow the summer season

5. What is unique about the Arctic tern's migration compared to other birds?

A. They migrate over land.
B. They travel the longest distance.
C. They fly in large groups.
D. They only fly during the night.

Reading Passage 6

Sarah was a young woman who loved to travel. She had visited many countries, but one place she had always wanted to explore was the Amazon rainforest. After saving enough money, Sarah finally booked a trip to South America.

When she arrived, Sarah joined a tour group led by an experienced guide. They hiked through dense forests, spotted rare animals like jaguars and colorful parrots, and listened to the sounds of the forest. The guide explained how important the rainforest was for the environment, as it produces much of the world's oxygen and is home to countless species of plants and animals.

During the trip, Sarah learned about the dangers the rainforest faces, such as deforestation and climate change. She returned home determined to help protect the environment and raise awareness about the need to conserve rainforests.

Questions for Reading Passage 6

1. Why had Sarah always wanted to visit the Amazon rainforest?

A. To meet new people
B. To explore a place she had never been
C. To become a tour guide
D. To move there someday

2. What did Sarah do after arriving in South America?

A. She visited a zoo.
B. She stayed in the city.
C. She joined a tour group to hike through the rainforest.
D. She got a job as a guide.

3. What did the guide explain about the rainforest?

A. It is only important for South America.
B. It is home to a few species of plants.
C. It has very few animals living in it.
D. It produces much of the world's oxygen.

4. What did Sarah learn during her trip?

A. Because this rainforest is in South America, protecting it is important only to people living in that continent.
B. Deforestation is good because it makes visiting the rainforest easier.
C. The rainforest faces dangers like deforestation and climate change.
D. It is easy to protect the rainforest.

5. What did Sarah decide to do after returning home?

A. Help protect the environment
B. Start her own tour company
C. Move to South America someday
D. Write a book about her travels

Reading Passage 7

Maria loved visiting the library every Saturday afternoon. She would spend hours browsing through the rows of books, trying to decide which ones to borrow. Her favorite section was the mystery novels, and she always tried to solve the mystery before the characters did.

One Saturday, the librarian, Mrs. Patel, noticed Maria had checked out more books than usual. "You must really love reading, Maria!" she said with a smile. Maria nodded and explained, "I'm entering a reading challenge at school. I need to read 10 books in a month, and I want to make sure I'm ready."

Mrs. Patel handed Maria a bookmark with tips on how to keep track of the books she read. Maria thanked her and left the library excited to start her reading challenge.

Questions for Reading Passage 7

1. What is Maria's favorite section in the library?
A. Science fiction   B. Mystery novels   C. History books   D. Adventure stories

2. Why did Maria check out more books than usual?
A. She was entering a reading challenge at school.
B. She wanted to read over the summer.
C. She was bored at home.
D. She needed to do research for a project.

3. What did Mrs. Patel give Maria?
A. A library card   C. A bookmark with tips
B. A new book   D. A list of mystery novels

4. How did Maria feel about the reading challenge?
A. Nervous   B. Frustrated   C. Bored   D. Excited

5. What does Maria try to do when reading mystery novels?
A. Finish them quickly
B. Avoid knowing the ending until she reads the entire book
C. Solve the mystery before the characters do
D. Write her own endings

Reading Passage 8

Every Saturday, Jack and his grandfather went fishing at the lake near their home. They would wake up early, pack their fishing rods and bait, and head out while the morning mist still hung over the water. Jack loved these quiet mornings, listening to the birds and watching the sun rise.

One Saturday, after an hour of fishing, Jack's line tugged hard. "I've got something!" he shouted excitedly. His grandfather helped him reel it in, and they pulled out a large fish. Jack beamed with pride.

"That's a big one," his grandfather said with a smile. "You're getting better every week." After releasing the fish back into the lake, they spent the rest of the morning quietly fishing, enjoying their time together.

Questions for Reading Passage 8

1. What do Jack and his grandfather do every Saturday?
A. Go swimming   B. Play baseball   C. Go hiking   D. Go fishing

2. Why did Jack shout?
A. He saw a large bird.   C. He saw a big fish in the lake.
B. He thought he may have caught a fish.   D. He dropped his rod in the lake.

3. What did Jack's grandfather say about the fish he caught?
A. "I've got something!"   C. "You're getting better every week."
B. "We need to keep it."   D. "Great job."

4. What did Jack and his grandfather do after catching the fish?
A. They released the fish back into the lake.   C. They went home.
B. They ate the fish.   D. They gave the fish to a friend.

5. Why did Jack enjoy these mornings at the lake?
A. He liked the quiet and watching the sunrise.
B. He liked seeing things he had never seen before at the lake.
C. He didn't have to do any work.
D. He loved swimming in the lake.

This is the end of this section.

Written Expression

- In this section, your child will be tested on their writing skills. This includes punctuation, grammar, word usage, verb tenses, and sentence structure.

- This section is 40 minutes and has two types of questions:

Question Type 1 (p.19-21)

- In the first part, your child will be given three (3) lines of a sentence/passage.

- Tell your child that they must become an "editor." They must <u>carefully</u> read the passage (as if they are an editor) looking for mistakes in punctuation, grammar, word usage, verb tenses, and sentence structure. Then, they mark the corresponding line (A, B, C) with the mistake.

- If there is no mistake, they mark D (no mistake).

Question Type 2 (p.22-28)

- In the second part, your child must read a longer passage, then answer questions about specific sentences in the passage.

Directions for Question Type 1 (p.19-21): Read the three lines of writing. They are marked A, B, and C. There may be a mistake in the writing. If there is a mistake, mark the choice with the mistake (A, B, or C). If there is not a mistake, then mark choice D (no mistakes).

Example Question

A) My brother lives in
B) Boston It is one of the
C) oldest cities in the country.
D) no mistakes

The answer is B. There should be a period at the end of the first sentence: My brother lives in Boston. It is one of the

1.
A) My brother and dad goes to the park
B) every Sunday to play soccer,
C) and they often meet friends there.
D) no mistakes

2.
A) Sarah and I has been best friends
B) since we were four. We always
C) have fun together on weekends.
D) no mistakes

3.
A) The kids were running through the park,
B) and one of them stepped in a puddle
C) with both of his foots.
D) no mistakes

4.
A) During the hike, we plan to
B) stop to take a break and
C) ate our snacks by the river.
D) no mistakes

5.
A) She was excited to see her cousins,
B) but her and her sister
C) arrived a little late.
D) no mistakes

6.
A) My uncle takes his car to get washed
B) every Saturday morning. He also
C) gets coffee with a friend afterward.
D) no mistakes

7.
A) Olivia loves reading books
B) about animals. She always brings
C) one to class to read during break.
D) no mistakes

8.
A) He left the backpacks in the car,
B) so they had to run back
C) before there game started.
D) no mistakes

9.
A) Emma ate nearly her sandwich
B) before she realized it was time
C) to head back to class.
D) no mistakes

10.
A) Be sure to grab your umbrella
B) before we leave for school,
C) or your going to get wet later.
D) no mistakes

11.
A) There is a park near my house
B) where many kids like to play.
C) The swings makes everyone want to go there.
D) no mistakes

12.
A) My cat enjoys sitting by the window.
B) This spot is her favorite place,
C) and it's always sunny there.
D) no mistakes

13.
A) The seat on my bike
B) breaked while I was riding.
C) My parents helped me fix it.
D) no mistakes

14.
A) Every time we visit the beach,
B) we see seagulls flying over
C) them waves in the ocean.
D) no mistakes

15.
A) The bookstore downtown has several
B) box's of new books that just arrived,
C) including the latest mystery novel.
D) no mistakes

Directions: Read the passage. Then, answer the questions below. There are small numbers in front of the sentences. For example: ¹We saw many... **These numbers help identify the sentences.**

Reading Passage for Questions 16-19

¹We saw many different exhibits at the museum, but my favorite part was the planetarium show. ²Our teacher explained how planets <u>move around the sun</u>. ³After the show, we got to ask questions.

⁴In the afternoon, we ate lunch at the park near the museum. ⁵My friend Max brought sandwiches, and I shared my chips with him. ⁶We had soccer practice that day after school.

⁷The whole day was <u>so much fun, and the entire class</u> is excited to visit the museum again.

Questions

16. Choose the best first sentence for this passage.
A. This year in science class we are studying plants, animals, and outer space.
B. My class went on a field trip to the city science museum yesterday.
C. Yesterday my mom dropped me off at school.
D. Next week, we will study the moon.

17. What is the best way to write the underlined part of sentence 2?
A. orbit around the sun
B. hover over the sun
C. fly around the sun
D. glide over the sun

18. Which sentence does not belong in the passage?
A. 2   B. 4   C. 6   D. 7

19. What is the best way to write the underlined part of sentence 7?
A. so much fun, but the entire class
B. so much fun, unless the entire class
C. so much fun so the entire class
D. no change

Reading Passage for Questions 20-23

¹My school hosted an Olympics Day last Friday. ²All the students were divided into teams, each representing a different country. ³My team represented Japan, and we had fun making our country's flag and wearing matching headbands. ⁴The day started with a parade, where each team marched around the field waving their flags. ⁵After the parade, we participated in the events. ⁶We participated in events such as races, relays, and even a tug-of-war competition. ⁷Last summer at camp, my team won the tug-of-war competition. ⁸At the end of the day, everyone gathered in the gym for the award ceremony.

Questions

20. What is the best way to write sentence 3?
A. My team represented Japan so we had fun making our country's flag, and headbands.
B. My team represented Japan, although we had fun making the country's flag and wearing headbands.
C. My team represented Japan, and had fun making our country's flag while wearing headbands.
D. no change

21. How can sentences 5 and 6 be combined?
A. After the parade, we participated in events such as races, relays, and a tug-of-war.
B. The parade happened before the events, with events such as races, relays, and tug-of-war.
C. The events, including races, relays, and tug-of-war, began after the parade.
D. After the parade, the events were all about races and relays before the tug-of-war.

22. Which sentence does not belong in the passage?
A. 4   B. 6   C. 7   D. 1

23. Choose the best way to end this passage.
A. We cheered for the winners and celebrated together.
B. The tug-of-war should have been the first event of the day.
C. I didn't enjoy the races, but the obstacle course was okay.
D. I wish we had won first place.

Reading Passage for Questions 24-27 ——————————————

[1]Our school had a charity bake sale recently. [2]The bake sale is organized by the student council, and all the money raised will go to a local animal shelter. [3]Each class was responsible for baking different treats, like cupcakes, brownies, and cookies. [4]Cookies are the most popular dessert in America. [5]After setting up our table, we started selling the treats to students, teachers, and parents. [6]By the end of the day, we sold all the treats and raised a lot of money. [7]I was proud of how hard everyone worked to make the bake sale a success. [8]My class made chocolate chip cookies, and I helped bake them with my friends. [9]Our teacher said we raised over $500 for the animal shelter.

Questions

24. What is the best way to write sentence 2?
A. The bake sale is organized the student council, and all the money raised will go to a local animal shelter.
B. The bake sale was organized by the student council, and all the money raised went to a local animal shelter.
C. The bake sale is organized by the student council, and all the money we raise will be going to a local animal shelter.
D. no change

25. Which sentence is out of order in the passage?
A. 3   B. 4   C. 6   D. 8

26. Which sentence does not belong in the passage?
A. 4   B. 6   C. 7   D. 9

27. Choose the best way to end this passage.
A. I wish we had raised more money for the animal shelter.
B. The bake sale started on Saturday at 11 A.M.
C. Our bake sale went so well that we already planned another one for next year.
D. I didn't enjoy baking, but at least we raised some money.

Reading Passage for Questions 28-31

¹My class took a field trip to Washington D.C. this past spring. ²It was an early morning bus ride, but we were all excited to explore the nation's capital. ³Our first stop was the National Mall, where we visited the Lincoln Memorial. ⁴Standing at the foot of the giant statue, I felt amazed by the history all around us. ⁵Afterward, we walked to the Washington Monument, and some of us took pictures with the tall structure in the background. ⁶At lunchtime, we ate sandwiches near the reflecting pool and enjoyed the view. ⁷In the afternoon, we visited the Smithsonian Museum of American History, which was full of interesting exhibits. ⁸My favorite exhibit was the display about the American presidents. ⁹We learned about different artifacts from past presidents, like Abraham Lincoln's hat and George Washington's sword. ¹⁰Last year, my dad dressed up as George Washington for Halloween. ¹¹After a long day of exploring, <u>we finally return to school. We are tired, but happy.</u>

Questions

28. What is the best way to write sentence 4?
A. I stood at the foot of the giant statue and am amazed by history all around us.
B. At the foot of the giant statue amazed by the history all around us was how I felt.
C. I stood at the foot of the giant statue I was amazed by the history all around us.
D. No change

29. What is the best way to write the underlined part of sentence 11?
A. we finally return, tired, happy.
B. we finally return to school, tired, but happy.
C. we finally returned to school. We were tired, but happy.
D. no change.

30. Which sentence does not belong in the paragraph?
A. 2   B. 5   C. 8   D. 10

31. Choose the best way to end this passage.
A. I felt excited for our next school trip.
B. The bus ride back was very quiet.
C. I didn't enjoy the museum as much as I thought I would.
D. I wish we could have spent more time at the Lincoln Memorial.

Reading Passage for Questions 32-35

[1]Last summer, I joined a soccer team for the first time. [2]At first, I was nervous because I had never played soccer before. [3]My coach taught us the basics, like passing, shooting dribbling and teamwork. [4]Every practice, I got a little better, and soon I was feeling more confident on the field. [5]My favorite position to play is forward because I get to try to score goals. [6]In our first game, I scored my very first goal, and my teammates cheered. [7]My parents took me out for ice cream because they didn't last night. [8]Playing soccer was a great way to make new friends. [9]Playing the sport was also a good way to stay active.

Questions

32. What is the best way to write sentence 3?
A. My coach teaches us the basics, like passing shooting dribbling and, teamwork.
B. My coach taught us the basics like passing, shooting, dribbling and, teamwork.
C. My coach taught us the basics, like passing, shooting, dribbling, and teamwork.
D. no change

33. Which sentence does not belong in the passage?
A. 2
B. 5
C. 7
D. 8

34. How can sentences 8 and 9 be combined?
A. Playing soccer has been a great way to make new friends and playing soccer has also been a good way to stay active.
B. Playing soccer has been a great way to make new friends and stay active.
C. Playing soccer has been a great way to make new friends, however playing the sport has also been a good way to stay active.
D. Playing soccer has been a great way to make new friends and on another note it has also been a good way to stay active.

35. Choose the best way to end this passage.

A. I planned to continue to play soccer and improve for next season.

B. Soccer is the most popular sport in the world.

C. Ice cream is a great reward for scoring a goal.

D. Playing forward is the best position in soccer.

This is the end of this section.

This page is intentionally left blank.

The Mathematics section begins on the next page.

Mathematics

- The Mathematics section consists 50 questions. Students have 30 minutes to complete this section.
- Some questions are simply text and numbers (questions 1-31), while others involve visuals (questions 32-50).
- Be sure your child:
  - does the correct operation (i.e., doesn't add, when the problem involves division)
  - circles/underlines important info in word problems
- If your child finds that they can't come up with an answer, they can test each answer choice. They can also use the process of elimination.

Directions: Read the question then choose the answer.

Example Questions

Which of these numbers is more than 82?

A. 79
B. 68
C. 59
D. 90

What would be the best estimation of this?   79 + 48

A. 100
B. 110
C. 130
D. 140

What would be the best estimation of this?   81 - 34

A. 50
B. 40
C. 60
D. 30

1. Which of the following groups contains only even numbers?

A. 48, 52, 106, 123, 258

B. 62, 60, 88, 142, 261

C. 24, 58, 92, 140, 208

D. 61, 77, 128, 220, 332

2. What would be the best estimation of this?   563 + 248

A. 900

B. 800

C. 700

D. 600

3. Which of these numbers is less than 63?

A. 89

B. 65

C. 59

D. 91

4. What number between 20 and 50 is a multiple of both 4 and 8?

A. 28

B. 40

C. 36

D. 44

5. Which unit is best to measure the weight of a pencil?

A. cup

B. kilogram

C. inch

D. gram

6. What would the weight of an apple be (approximately)?

A. 50 ounces
B. 8 ounces
C. 5 pounds
D. 2000 grams

7. Which of these would weigh the closest to 4 pounds?

A. a slice of bread
B. a carrot
C. a laptop
D. a car tire

8. What is 3,000 + 600 + 7 written in standard form?

A. 3,067
B. 3,670
C. 3,076
D. 3,607

9. John started reading his book at 2:30 p.m. He read for one and a half hours Fifteen minutes before he finished reading, his sister called him. What time was it when his sister called?

A. 3:45
B. 4:00
C. 4:15
D. 3:30

10. Sarah likes to collect marbles. During her first year of collecting them, she collected 200 marbles. During her second year, she collected another 150 marbles, but, unfortunately, she lost 30 of them. Which answer choice represents the number of marbles Sarah had at the end of the second year?

A. 150 + 30 - 200
B. 200 - 150 + 30
C. 200 - (150 - 30)
D. 200 + 150 - 30

11. A number pattern starts with 14 and ends with 42. Which rule is best for this pattern?

A. skip count by 3s
B. skip count by 5s
C. skip count by 7s
D. skip count by 9s

12. What one of the answer choices is the smallest fraction?

A. 5/9
B. 5/7
C. 5/5
D. 5/3

13. What is the answer to this problem: 7/20 + 3/20 - 5/20 = ?

A. 5/20
B. 15/20
C. 5/40
D. 5/60

14. Anna likes to collect seashells at the beach. On Tuesday she collects 8 seashells. On the remaining days, she collects 5 seashells each day. How many seashells will she have at the end of the day on Friday?

A. 20
B. 23
C. 25
D. 28

15. In the number sentence below, what sign would replace the question mark?
$$45 \div (10 \; ? \; 2) = 9$$

A. $+$
B. $-$
C. $\div$
D. $\times$

16. Which of the following expressions is equivalent to $(5 \times 8) \times 3 + 5$?

A. $(5 + 5) \times 3 + 8$
B. $5 + 3 \times (8 + 5)$
C. $(8 \times 3) \times 5 + 5$
D. $(3 \times 5) \times 8 + 3$

17. Which of these tools is best for measuring the length of a see-saw?

A. scale
B. thermometer
C. ruler
D. tape measure

18. Which of the following has a temperature closest to 20°F?

A. inside a refrigerator
B. a warm day in summer
C. hot tea
D. a snowy day in winter

19. Solve for Y.

$$Y + 5 = 9$$

A. 3

B. 4

C. 5

D. 9

20. The height of a rose bush in Maria's garden is 15.7 inches. The height of a rose bush in Tom's garden is 11.4 inches. What is the difference between the heights of the two rose bushes?

A. 4.3 in

B. 5.3 in

C. 4.1 in

D. 3.9 in

21. The product of 154 × 4 would be _____.

A. between 400 and 500

B. between 500 and 600

C. between 600 and 700

D. between 700 and 800

22. Mel's fishbowl already contained 8 cups of water. Mel added more water until the fishbowl reached its capacity of 15 cups. Which expression represents the amount of water, in cups, Mel added to the fishbowl?

A. $15 \div 8$

B. $15 - 8$

C. $8 + 15$

D. 8×15

23. **Lara has 240 stickers. She needs to arrange them into notebooks. Each notebook must contain the same amount of stickers. How many notebooks should Lara use?**

A. 6 notebooks
B. 9 notebooks
C. 11 notebooks
D. 14 notebooks

24. **Which would be the best unit to measure the weight of a pickup truck?**

A. gram
B. liter
C. ton
D. meter

25. **Which number sentence would have even result?**

A. 121 - 56
B. 200 - 99
C. 84 - 45
D. 135 – 63

26. **Sam has 52 books, which he organizes in several shelves. Each shelf has space for 9 books. How many shelves does Sam need for all of his books?**

A. 5
B. 6
C. 15
D. 24

27. Which answer choice has this: six ten-thousands, four thousands, three fewer hundreds than thousands, two more tens than hundreds, and five ones?

A. 64,135

B. 64,325

C. 64,425

D. 64,245

28. There are 10 students. These 10 students were sitting together at a lunch table. Then, 3 stood up and left the table. What fraction of all the students continued sitting at the table?

A. 3/10

B. 7/10

C. 1/3

D. 1/2

29. Which of the following inequalities is true?

A. $28 + 15 > 40 + 7$

B. $50 - 22 < 18 - 60$

C. $45 - 20 < 70 - 35$

D. $46 + 12 < 20 + 30$

30. There are 4 kids: Emily, Sarah, Jack, and Mark. They want to sit on a bench next to each other at the park. If Emily decides to sit on the rightmost side of the bench, how many different ways do Sarah, Jack, and Mark have to sit down on this bench?

A. 2

B. 6

C. 3

D. 9

31. The height of a third grader is most likely between

A. 1 and 2 feet
B. 3 and 5 yards
C. 20 and 25 inches
D. 50 and 55 inches

32. Which answer choice best describes this shape?

A. a polygon and a rhombus
B. a polygon and a parallelogram
C. a polygon and a pentagon
D. a quadrilateral and a trapezoid

33. Which one of the answer choices is true?

A.   >

B.   =

C.   >

D.   <

34. Find the volume of the object below in cubic units.

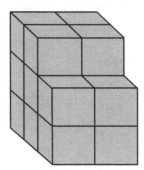

A. 12 cubic units
B. 14 cubic units
C. 15 cubic units
D. 16 cubic units

35. What is the area of the gray part below?

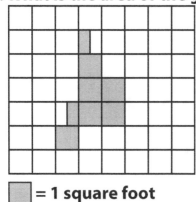

= 1 square foot

A. 7 square feet
B. 6 square feet
C. 8 square feet
D. 5 square feet

36. What number should go in the box below?

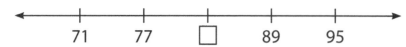

71   77   ☐   89   95

A. 82
B. 83
C. 84
D. 85

37. Which shape does <u>not</u> have a line of symmetry?

A.

B.

C.

D.

38. Which picture shows a quadrilateral?

A.

B.

C.

D.

39. The perimeter of the shape below is 80 in. Find the missing value for "X".

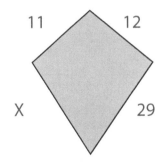

A. 28
B. 29
C. 27
D. 15

40. What is the perimeter of the gray figure below?

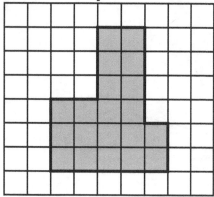

| = 1 unit

A. 22 units

B. 20 units

C. 18 units

D. 30 units

41. Lee has a group of stickers. The group of stickers is shown here. First, Lee picked one sticker with a basketball. She put this sticker away in her desk. Now, without looking, Lee will pick another sticker. Of the stickers that are left, which one is she most likely to pick?

A. ![basketball]

B. ![sun]

C. ![star]

D. ![cupcake]

42. The chart below shows each kid's number of pets. What is the mean number of pets?

    A. 3
    B. 2
    C. 12
    D. 24

Kid	Number of Pets
Jess	5
Mark	2
Alex	2
Miley	3
Kevin	1
Rob	2
Tara	5
Mike	4

43. Here is the same chart as Question 42. What is the mode?

    A. 3
    B. 2
    C. 5
    D. 24

Kid	Number of Pets
Jess	5
Mark	2
Alex	2
Miley	3
Kevin	1
Rob	2
Tara	5
Mike	4

44. Here is the same chart as Question 42. What is the range?

   A. 5
   B. 4
   C. 3
   D. 2

Kid	Number of Pets
Jess	5
Mark	2
Alex	2
Miley	3
Kevin	1
Rob	2
Tara	5
Mike	4

45.

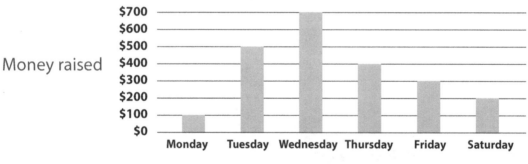

The amount of money raised for the animal shelter fundraiser

The Franklin Animal Shelter is raising money during a fundraiser this week. The animal shelter estimates that the amount of money raised on Sunday will be $700. According to this estimate, how much more money will be raised on Sunday than on Tuesday?

   A. $0
   B. $100
   C. $200
   D. $300

46. Using the graph from Question 44, what was the total amount of money raised on Monday, Tuesday, and Thursday?

A. $300

B. $600

C. $900

D. $1,000

47. Using the graph from Question 44, what was the total amount of money raised on Monday, Tuesday, Wednesday, Thursday, Friday, and Saturday?

A. $ 2,200

B. $ 2,100

C. $ 2,000

D. $ 1,900

48.

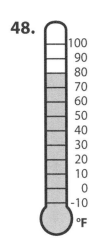

This is a thermometer showing the temperature in Atlanta. The temperature in Miami is 10 degrees warmer than the temperature in Atlanta. What is the temperature in Miami?

A. 80 degrees

B. 90 degrees

C. 70 degrees

D. 100 degrees

49. Which shape has the most line segments?

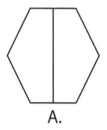   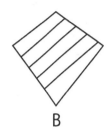   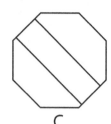   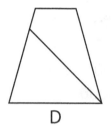

A.　　　　　　B　　　　　　C　　　　　　D

50. Which one of the below shapes does <u>not</u> have a right angle?

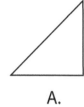　　　　　　　　　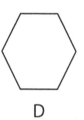

A.　　　　　　B　　　　　　C　　　　　　D

This is the end of this section.

Vocabulary

- This section consists of 30 questions testing your child's vocabulary.

- Students have 15 minutes to complete this section.

- After reading the short phrase, your child must choose which word or phrase has the same/almost the same meaning as the underlined word.

- Carefully read the brief phrase, paying close attention to the underlined word.

- Try to come up with a simple definition of the underlined word. Some words have more than one definition, so be sure that it fits with the phrase you just read.

- Remember, the correct answer may either be a word with the exact same meaning as the underlined word or one with simply a very similar meaning (but not exact).

Directions: Read the short phrase. Look at the underlined word. Choose the answer that means the same thing-or close to the same thing-as the underlined word.

Example Question

1. a frigid temperature

A. very cold
B. mild
C. very hot
D. changing

The answer is A. (Frigid means very cold.)

1. a sponge can absorb

A. push away
B. soak up
C. lose
D. block

2. approach the building

A. leave
B. climb
C. beat
D. move toward

3. consider what happened

A. forget
B. ignore
C. think about
D. enjoy

4. to contain liquid

A. hold
B. release
C. drink
D. mix

5. a vase that is delicate

A. sturdy
B. beautiful
C. easily broken
D. simple

6. a painting that is ancient

A. new
B. very old
C. fake
D. colorful

7. the plant will decay

A. grow
B. weaken
C. disappear
D. rot

8. to rely on a friend

A. depend
B. cheer
C. focus
D. call

9. a swift response

A. slow
B. quick
C. wrong
D. correct

10. to digest food

A. smell
B. cook
C. taste
D. break down

11. recall an event

A. remember
B. forget
C. plan
D. attend

12. a frail tree

A. large
B. tall
C. weak
D. heavy

13. a gradual change

A. quick
B. slow
C. big
D. surprising

14. they intend to

A. forget
B. hate
C. want
D. plan

15. the primary idea

A. second
B. popular
C. main
D. last

16. the solution

A. trouble
B. answer
C. question
D. number

17. a new theory

A. fact
B. ending
C. show
D. idea

18. to triumph in a contest

A. win
B. compete
C. lose
D. judge

19. a fortunate event

A. lucky
B. serious
C. surprising
D. happy

20. a distant memory

A. recent
B. far off
C. strong
D. forgotten

21. a brief video

A. quiet
B. long
C. new
D. short

22. to examine the book

A. put back
B. read aloud
C. look carefully at
D. read quietly

23. to imitate the sound

A. copy
B. record
C. listen to
D. follow

24. to locate the shop

A. go into
B. paint
C. find
D. like

25. a mystifying answer

A. simple
B. confusing
C. short
D. wrong

26. she will confess the reason

A. lie about
B. explain
C. hide
D. tell

27. a typical day

A. strange
B. warm
C. normal
D. boring

28. to occur at night

A. happen
B. disappear
C. get dark
D. end

29. a diagram of the room

A. model
B. photo
C. video
D. drawing

30. to irritate your classmate

A. calm
B. bother
C. help
D. ignore

This is the end of this section.

Spelling

- This section consists of 24 questions testing your child's spelling skills.
- After looking at each answer choice, your child must choose which word is not spelled correctly.
- Be sure your child carefully reads each word.
- Here, your child acts as an "editor" once again, carefully scanning for mistakes. Keep a lookout for mistakes like: missing letters, extra letters that are not needed, and switched letters.
- Students have 15 minutes to complete this section.

Directions: Read the four words (choice A, B, C, and D). If one of these is not spelled correctly, mark the one that is not spelled correctly. If all of the words (choice A, B, C, and D) are spelled correctly, then mark choice E (no mistakes).

Example Questions

Ex1. A. believe
 B. friend
 C. becuase
 D. honest
 E. (no mistakes)

Ex2. A. repeat
 B. snail
 C. honor
 D. elastic
 E. (no mistakes)

Answers: C (because); E (no mistakes)

1. A. leave
    B. waved
    C. afraid
    D. bookes
    E. (no mistakes)

6. A. libraryies
    B. picture
    C. elephant
    D. easily
    E. (no mistakes)

2. A. catch
    B. great
    C. allways
    D. easy
    E. (no mistakes)

7. A. collect
    B. usually
    C. uniform
    D. meen
    E. (no mistakes)

3. A. throne
    B. often
    C. sutch
    D. almost
    E. (No mistakes)

8. A. beautiful
    B. gess
    C. library
    D. quickly
    E. (no mistakes)

4. A. blew
    B. above
    C. human
    D. boath
    E. (no mistakes)

9. A. stirred
    B. danger
    C. jurie
    D. laid
    E. (no mistakes)

5. A. zipper
    B. aded
    C. animal
    D. plastic
    E. (no mistakes)

10. A. guard
    B. given
    C. raise
    D. babies
    E. (no mistakes)

11. A. taught
    B. liar
    C. orphan
    D. fourty
    E. (no mistakes)

12. A. wrapper
    B. doller
    C. happiest
    D. hospital
    E. (no mistakes)

13. A. brother
    B. weight
    C. quickly
    D. funiest
    E. (no mistakes)

14. A. ghost
    B. favorit
    C. shield
    D. wonderful
    E. (no mistakes)

15. A. once
    B. stare
    C. fastest
    D. piece
    E. (no mistakes)

16. A. sicknes
    B. thousand
    C. mistake
    D. river
    E. (no mistakes)

17. A. doubel
    B. purple
    C. squeeze
    D. scramble
    E. (no mistakes)

18. A. wrinkle
    B. scream
    C. explain
    D. everything
    E. (no mistakes)

19. A. crooked
    B. calmlly
    C. reuse
    D. undo
    E. (no mistakes)

20. A. stubborn
    B. taught
    C. beyond
    D. whissle
    E. (no mistakes)

21.　A. crowd
　　　B. fortune
　　　C. quik
　　　D. coward
　　　E. (no mistakes)

22.　A. mountain
　　　B. hooves
　　　C. jawbone
　　　D. ought
　　　E. (no mistakes)

23.　A. arrow
　　　B. botom
　　　C. wisdom
　　　D. useful
　　　E. (no mistakes)

24.　A. saving
　　　B. soke
　　　C. tried
　　　D. countries
　　　E. (no mistakes)

This is the end of this section.

Capitalization

- This section consists of 20 questions testing your child's knowledge of capitalization rules.

- Your child will read a sentence or brief passage, looking for capitalization errors.

- Be sure your child carefully reads each line of the question. Here, your child acts as an "editor" once again, carefully scanning for mistakes.

- Students have 10 minutes to complete this section.

Directions: Read the three lines (choice A, B, and C) and look for capitalization mistakes. A word could be missing a capital letter. Or, a word may have a capital letter where it does not need one. If you find a mistake, mark the letter of the line that has the mistake. If there are no mistakes, mark choice D (no mistakes).

Example Questions

Ex1. A. My favorite month is december.
B. It usually snows a lot that time of year.
C. I love to build snowmen and go sledding.
D. (no mistakes)

Ex2. A. My brother thinks spring is the best season.
B. He thinks the weather is great.
C. Plus, he likes that he has one week off from school.
D. (no mistakes)

Answers: A (December); D (no mistakes)

1. A. My family is going to have a picnic at the park on saturday.
    B. We are bringing sandwiches and chips, plus a kite
    C. to play with after we eat lunch.
    D. (no mistakes)

2. A. We are going to visit my friend next week.
    B. He lives in chicago, which is a big city.
    C. I always have fun when I go there.
    D. (no mistakes)

3. A. On our trip to Washington, D.C., we visited many famous landmarks.
    B. One of the highlights was seeing the lincoln Memorial.
    C. We learned a lot about American history during our visit.
    D. (no mistakes)

4. A. We went on a hike in the Mountains last weekend.
    B. It was a beautiful day, and we saw many animals.
    C. When we reached the top, we had a picnic.
    D. (no mistakes)

5. A. Sarah enjoys reading books in the park.
    B. She usually brings a blanket to sit on
    C. and apples to eat while she reads.
    D. (no mistakes)

6. A. The tallest point in north America
    B. is Mount Denali, located in Alaska.
    C. It stands over twenty thousand feet tall.
    D. (no mistakes)

7. A. We are planning a family barbecue for
    B. memorial day. Everyone will bring their
    C. favorite dish to share with the group.
    D. (no mistakes)

8.   A. Brownies, Cookies, and Cakes
     B. were available at the bake sale
     C. at Washington Elementary.
     D. (no mistakes)

9.   A. Heading north, you will arrive at the Rocky Mountains,
     B. a major range that stretches
     C. across the western part of this continent.
     D. (no mistakes)

10. A. The art magazine I
     B. subscribe to is printed
     C. in Paris, france.
     D. (no mistakes)

11. A. Last night, my parents drove to the store
     B. to get groceries. as they drove, they passed
     C. several Ford trucks parked on the street.
     D. (no mistakes)

12. A. My sister and I just got a new puppy.
     B. We decided to name him max after our favorite movie.
     C. He loves to run around the yard and play fetch.
     D. (no mistakes)

13. A. The Grand Canyon is a popular tourist spot.
     B. Many people visit each year to see the beautiful views.
     C. The Grand Canyon is also known for its history.
     D. (no mistakes)

14. A. Traveling south, you will find the Amazon River,
     B. which flows through Brazil and is
     C. one of the longest rivers in the world.
     D. (no mistakes)

15. A. In 1492, Explorer Christopher Columbus sailed across
     B. the Atlantic Ocean in search of a new route to Asia.
     C. His voyage is one of the most famous in history.
     D. (no mistakes)

16. A. My aunt loves fancy jewelry.
     B. Each weekend she goes to a store called
     C. "hidden treasures" to buy more.
     D. (no mistakes)

17. A. My dad is an excellent cook. He
     B. was born in Italy and moved to the u.s.
     C. when he was a teenager.
     D. (no mistakes)

18. A. I think *the wizard of oz*
     B. was the most famous movie
     C. directed by Victor Fleming.
     D. (no mistakes)

19. A. Next, my sister and I are
     B. going to Ramon Plaza to get some
     C. cookies from our neighbor's, kerry's, bakery.
     D. (no mistakes)

20. A. Dear Mrs. Johnson,
     B. I hope you had a great weekend.
     C. Sincerely Yours, Emma
     D. (no mistakes)

This is the end of this section.

Punctuation

- This section consists of 20 questions testing your child's knowledge of punctuation rules.

- Your child will read a sentence or brief passage, looking for punctuation errors, once again as an "editor."

- Be sure your child carefully reads each line of the question.

- Students have 10 minutes to complete this section.

Directions: Read the three lines (choice A, B, and C), looking for punctuation mistakes. A sentence could be missing a punctuation mark. Or, a sentence may have a punctuation mark where it does not need one. If you find a mistake, mark the letter of the line that has the mistake. If there are no mistakes, mark choice D (no mistakes).

Example Questions

Ex1.　A. My favorite dessert is chocolate ice cream
　　　B. I could eat chocolate ice cream every day!
　　　C. My second favorite dessert is chocolate cake.
　　　D. (no mistakes)

Ex2.　A. My sister loves fruit smoothies.
　　　B. Her favorite things to add are strawberries, and bananas.
　　　C. Sometimes she also adds pineapple.
　　　D. (no mistakes)

Answers: A. My favorite dessert is chocolate ice cream.
B. Her favorite things to add are strawberries and bananas.

1. A) Sarah's favorite subjects
    B) in school are math science,
    C) and history.
    D) (no mistakes)

2. A) George Washington, the first
    B) president of the United States, was
    C) born on February 22 1732.
    D) (no mistakes)

3. A) Are you going to the
    B) school play tomorrow? No I have
    C) a family picnic to attend.
    D) (no mistakes)

4. A) Polar bears, and moose live in cold climates.
    B) Polar bears are excellent swimmers. They are
    C) well adapted to cold environments.
    D) (no mistakes)

5. A) John is a talented
    B) musician. He enjoys playing the
    C) piano writing songs and performing at local events.
    D) (no mistakes)

6. A) A science fair will be
    B) held at Riverside Elementary
    C) School in May 2026.
    D) (no mistakes)

7. A) We'll have to wait
    B) until the next bus comes.
    C) I cant believe we missed it.
    D) (no mistakes)

8. A) Do you think humans will
B) ever live on another planet
C) besides Earth? Only time will tell.
D) (no mistakes)

9. A) The principal announced that
B) our guest speaker will be
C) Mr Johnson, a famous scientist.
D) (no mistakes)

10. A) In my geography class, we studied
B) the countries that are famous for their history, like
C) Egypt Greece and China.
D) (no mistakes)

11. A) My brother is planning to
B) start a new job next Monday. He thinks
C) it will be fun, but he's not sure?
D) (no mistakes)

12. A) The Great Wall of China is one of the most famous landmarks. in
B) the world. It stretches over 13,000 miles
C) across northern China.
D) (no mistakes)

13. A) We have to go to the
B) new clinic on Maple Street.
C) Dr Smith is the head doctor there.
D) (no mistakes)

14. A) My sister was born
B) on December, 31 2010.
C) She was born on the last day of the year.
D) (no mistakes)

15. A) This weekend, we're planning to
B) go hiking. We'll visit
C) the mountains. Im really excited.
D) (no mistakes)

16. A) The library is next to the
B) town square Sarah and
C) Emily often meet there to study.
D) (no mistakes)

17. A) Can you see that, There's
B) an airplane. I can't tell
C) for sure because it's so far away.
D) (no mistakes)

18. A) Are you planning to go
B) to the park later? I heard
C) it's going to be sunny.
D) (no mistakes)

19. A) The students stayed up
B) late. to finish their homework
C) by the due date.
D) (no mistakes)

20. A) Sarah loves to read books in
B) the evening She usually
C) reads for an hour before bed.
D) (no mistakes)

This is the end of this section.

Computation (Mathematics)

- This section consists of 26 questions testing your child's mathematics skills, specifically in computing (adding, subtracting, multiplying, and dividing).
- Be sure your child carefully looks at the sign(s) in each question and does not make a careless mistake by performing the wrong operation.
- Scratch paper is allowed. Students can use it to perform calculations instead of trying to do them in their head. Mistakes are less likely this way.
- Students have 20 minutes to complete this section.
- Below is a simple example.

Directions: Solve the math problem. Then, find and mark your answer. If your answer is not shown, then mark choice D. Choice D has the letter "N." ("N" means "not given," as in "your answer was not given.")

Example Questions ————————————————————————

Ex1. 15 + 25 =

A. 30
B. 40
C. 50
D. N

Ex2. 40 – 17 =

A. 33
B. 37
C. 27
D. N

Answers: B, D

1. 15 + 22 =

A. 37
B. 27
C. 42
D. N

2. 48 – 19 =

A. 31
B. 30
C. 29
D. N

3. 7 × 6 =

A. 42
B. 13
C. 48
D. N

4. 81 ÷ 8 =

A. 7
B. 8
C. 9
D. N

5. 48 ÷ 6 =

A. 8
B. 7
C. 6
D. N

6. 435 - 78 = ?

A. 513
B. 357
C. 367
D. N

7. 378 + 43 = ?

A. 421
B. 411
C. 335
D. N

8. 150 × 3 =

A. 153
B. 300
C. 450
D. N

9. 823 - 149 = ?

A. 674
B. 972
C. 684
D. N

10. 389 + 46 = ?

A. 425
B. 445
C. 343
D. N

11. 592 - 247 = ?

A. 349
B. 839
C. 345
D. N

12. 34 × 6 =

A. 204
B. 184
C. 214
D. N

13. 360 ÷ 10 =

A. 360
B. 350
C. 370
D. N

14. 27 + 46 + 38 = ?

A. 105
B. 110
C. 115
D. N

15. 4 × 120 =

A. 480
B. 124
C. 484
D. N

16. 5 × 312 =

A. 1,570
B. 1,560
C. 1,596
D. N

17. 39 + 50 + 7 = ?

A. 86
B. 96
C. 76
D. N

18. 23 + 35 + 128 = ?

A. 186
B. 176
C. 196
D. N

19. 542 - 96 = ?

A. 456
B. 638
C. 554
D. N

20. 629 - 154 = ?

A. 475
B. 535
C. 575
D. N

21. 326 + 187

A. 503
B. 513
C. 139
D. N

22. 7 × 3 × 9 =

A. 19
B. 189
C. 119
D. N

23. 1800 ÷ 6 = ?

A. 370
B. 270
C. 420
D. N

24. 2400 ÷ 8 = ?

A. 300
B. 320
C. 340
D. N

25. 240 ÷ 12 = ?

A. 18
B. 20
C. 22
D. N

26. 5025 ÷ 25 = ?

A. 101
B. 21
C. 201
D. N

This is the end of this section.

Word Analysis

- **Note: you must read the questions to your child in this section. See page 89.**
- Your child will be read a word or part of a word. Then, they must choose an answer based on the prompt you read to them.
- Be sure your child listens very carefully as you read the question.
- Below are three examples. The material to read to your child is on page 89.

Directions: Listen carefully, then choose your answer.

Example Questions

Example 1

A. fishing
B. secret
C. shovel
D. crash

Example 2

A. 1
B. 2
C. 3
D. 0

Example 3

A. fraid
B. fr
C. af
D. un

Answers: C, B, D

1. A. kite
   B. guitar
   C. table
   D. sugar

2. A. chest
   B. cast
   C. catch
   D. circle

3. A. talent
   B. trap
   C. bath
   D. think

4. A. flat
   B. sight
   C. bike
   D. late

5. A. fun
   B. fan
   C. bin
   D. fond

6. A. ft
   B. pt
   C. ra
   D. af

7. A. shampoo
   B. mass
   C. cash
   D. fast

8. A. u
   B. i
   C. e
   D. a

9. A. re
   B. refl
   C. ect
   D. lect

10. A. baby
    B. never
    C. photo
    D. tulip

11. A. 1
    B. 2
    C. 3
    D. 4

12. A. 1
    B. 2
    C. 3
    D. 4

13. A. mask
    B. teen
    C. wink
    D. muscle

14. A. seem
    B. tusk
    C. sail
    D. sign

15. A. thumb
    B. glitter
    C. insect
    D. follow

16. A. hippo
    B. sword
    C. monkey
    D. flash

17. A. hope
    B. ful
    C. hop
    D. ope

18. A. in a kind way
    B. a kind person
    C. the quality of being kind
    D. a kind action

19. A. pen
    B. dent
    C. de
    D. ind

20. A. still
    B. ness
    C. ill
    D. ss

21. A. sho
    B. ove
    C. vel
    D. ovel

22. A. bot
    B. tle
    C. ottle
    D. le

23. A. tele
    B. vision
    C. sion
    D. shan

24. A. happiness
    B. plastic
    C. fossil
    D. sunlight

25. A. insect
    B. thunder
    C. doorknob
    D. easily

26. A. any, body
    B. an, body
    C. anybody, one
    D. an, by, body

27. A. written
    B. writing
    C. writer
    D. write

28. A.    B.    C.    D.

29. A.    B.   C. 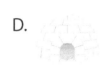   D.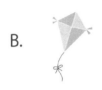

30. A.   B.    C.    D.

31. A.   B.   C.    D.

32. A.   B.   C.    D.

33. A.   B.   C.   D.

Listening

- **Note: you must read the questions to your child in this section. See page 90.**

- Your child will be read a brief story. Then, they will answer a question based on the information in the story.

- Be sure your child listens very carefully. They must focus on listening <u>and</u> memorizing what is being said.

- To practice listening skills, after you read the question to your child, have them repeat back to you what you just read. (Note that some questions will give information that is not necessary to answer the question.)

- Below is a simple example of a Listening question.

Example Questions

Example 1

A. measure
B. buy
C. compare
D. substitute

Example 2

A.    B.

C.    D.

Answers: B, B

1. A. The leaves will begin to change color.
   B. The leaves will stay in the trees.
   C. The leaves will blow into the yard.
   D. Maya will play in the leaves.

2. A. Monday
   B. Wednesday
   C. Thursday
   D. Friday

3. A. Max ran to the spot on the floor where the food had dropped.
   B. Max laid down on the floor in the hall.
   C. Ethan ignored Max and washed his hands.
   D. Ethan sat down at the table to finish his dinner.

4. A. orange juice
   B. water
   C. a smoothie
   D. milk

5. A. thought of
   B. touched
   C. ignored
   D. came near

6. A. answers
   B. measurements
   C. oceans
   D. experiments

7. A. a dinosaur statue
   B. a model of outer space
   C. the cafeteria
   D. the gift shop

8. A. pick up branches
B. water the flowers
C. sweep the porch
D. pull up weeds

9. A. 4
B. 5
C. 6
D. 8

10. A. 9-1-1
B. a park ranger
C. an ambulance
D. the police of the nearest town

11. A. walked around looking at plants
B. picked out some colorful flowers
C. paid at the cashier
D. planted the flowers in the garden

12. A. Kelly will be on time for her tennis lesson.
B. Kelly will sleep in for another hour.
C. Kelly will miss just a few minutes of her lesson.
D. Kelly will miss a lot of her tennis lesson.

13. A.  B.  C.  D.

14. A. B. C. D.

15. A.  B.  C.  D.

16. A.  B. C. D.

17. A.  B.  C. D.

18. A. B.  C. D.

19. A. B.   C.  D.

20. A. a fishing hat
B. mittens
C. swim shorts
D. boots

21. A. tree - flower - ant - bee

B. bee - tree - ant - flower

C. flower - bee - ant - tree

D. flower - tree - ant - bee

22. A.

B.

C.

D.

23. A.

B.

C.

D.

24. A.  B.  C. D.

25. A. B. C. D.

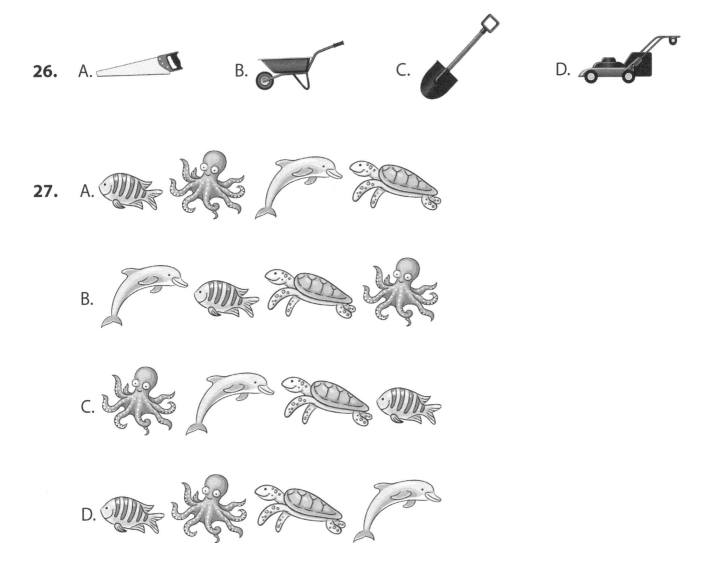

26. A.   B.   C.   D.

27. A.

B.

C.

D.

This is the end of this section.

Science

- This section evaluates your child's knowledge of scientific concepts and scientific terms.

- Allow approximately 30 minutes for this section.

Directions: Listen carefully, then choose your answer.

Example Question

What is the last step in the scientific method?

A. Do research.
B. Conduct an experiment.
C. Draw a conclusion.
D. Ask a question.

The answer is C.

1. In order to support their claims, scientists should have good sources of evidence. Which one of these is an example of a good source of evidence?

A. Test results
B. A best guess
C. An opinion expressed in a newspaper
D. A detailed comment about a video posted online

2. Which one of the below sentences are true about liquids?

A. They have closely packed particles.
B. They have a definite shape.
C. They take the shape of the container that they are in.
D. They can be firm and hard.

3. Which one of the below sentences are true about solids?

A. They have closely packed particles.
B. They have loosely packed particles.
C. They flow easily.
D. They have particles that move around.

4. What kind of object would a magnet attract?

A. An object made of plastic
B. An object made of steel
C. An object made of rubber
D. An object made of paper

5. Which of the events below is an example of a <u>fast</u> change to the Earth's surface?

A. weathering
B. glacier melting
C. earthquake
D. erosion

6. Which of the events below is <u>not</u> an example of a <u>fast</u> change to the Earth's surface?

A. landslide
B. tsunami
C. earthquake
D. erosion

7. The life cycle of which animal group includes laying eggs in water?

A. mammal
B. bird
C. reptile
D. amphibian

8. Which animal group can undergo a complete metamorphosis?

A. insect
B. mammal
C. bird
D. reptile

9. The life cycle of which animal group includes feeding babies milk?

A. insect
B. mammal
C. bird
D. reptile

10. The sun, together with eight planets, 146 moons, and a few dwarf planets, make up our _____.

A. universe
B. Milky Way
C. solar system
D. galaxy

11. Which planet is the hottest in our solar system?

A. Earth
B. Mars
C. Venus
D. Jupiter

12. The planet Mars has water. This water is in the form of ___ .

A. ice
B. a few lakes
C. rain drops
D. an ocean

13. Moon phases are the different shapes of the Moon that we see during different times of the month. Why do we see these phases?

A. Eclipses that occur nightly
B. Different amounts of light coming from the Earth
C. Different amounts of light coming from the Moon
D. From Earth, we only see the lit part of the Moon as it rotates around Earth

14. The moon appears to move across the sky at night. Why is this?

A. the Moon moves closer to the Sun
B. the Moon moves far away from Earth
C. the Earth rotates on its axis
D. the view of the Moon is blocked by clouds

15. The movement of Earth on its axis called ___ .

A. spherical force
B. rotation
C. vibration
D. interval force

16. The process of matter changing from a solid to a liquid is called ___.

A. melting
B. gas
C. evaporation
D. condensation

17. The process of matter changing from a liquid to a gas is called ___.

A. melting
B. gas
C. evaporation
D. condensation

18. Which of the following sentences explain how water is _different_ from other substances?

A. Water can change forms from a liquid to a solid.
B. Water can change forms from a liquid to a gas.
C. Water is less dense as a solid than liquid.
D. Water is more dense as a solid than a liquid.

19. Which one is _not_ a way that matter changes phases?

A. condensation
B. mixing
C. freezing
D. melting

20. What is the melting point of water?

A. 0 degrees Celsius
B. 32 degrees Celsius
C. 50 degrees Celsius
D. 100 degrees Celsius

21. Which part of the plant structure is meant to attract pollinators?

A. stem
B. flower
C. root
D. fruit

22. Which part of the plant structure collects sunlight for photosynthesis?

A. leaf
B. fruit
C. root
D. fertilizer

23. Which part of the plant structure collects water from the soil, minerals from soil, and helps to hold the plant to the ground?

A. stem
B. leaf
C. root
D. anchor

24. Which part of the plant structure brings nutrients and water up and down and also helps to hold the plant up?

A. stem
B. leaf
C. root
D. anchor

25. Which animal is the best example of a pollinator?

A. catfish
B. algae
C. tick
D. moth

This is the end of this section.

Social Studies

- This section evaluates your child's knowledge of social studies, particularly in the areas of government, history, economics, and geography.

- Allow approximately 30 minutes for this section.

Directions: Listen carefully, then choose your answer.

Example Question

Name three countries in North America.

A. America, Brazil, Canada
B. Canada, United States, Mexico
C. Alaska, Texas, California
D. New York, Canada, Mexico

The answer is B.

GOVERNMENT

1. What are the three branches of the federal government?

A. executive, state, democratic
B. executive, legislative, judicial
C. federal, state, local
D. democratic, executive, republic

2. The U.S. president is the leader of one of the government branches. Which one?

A. judicial
B. democratic
C. executive
D. electoral

3. The U.S. Congress is divided into two parts. What are their names?

A. House of Representatives and the Senate
B. Parliament and Council
C. President and the Supreme Court
D. Department of State and the Justice Department

4. The Supreme Court is part of which branch of government?

A. executive
B. legislative
C. judicial
D. electoral

5. Voters in states elect governors to lead which branch of state government?

A. council
B. departmental
C. judicial
D. executive

HISTORY

6. On what date did the 13 colonies declare their independence from Britain?

A. July 4, 1812
B. July 4, 1781
C. July 4, 1492
D. July 4, 1776

7. How many years did the Civil War last?

A. 4
B. 1
C. 7
D.10

8. Who was president during the Civil War?

A. Thomas Jefferson
B. Abraham Lincoln
C. John Adams
D. John F. Kennedy

9. Who was one of the leaders of the Underground Railroad?

A. Susan B. Anthony
B. Harriet Tubman
C. Sandra Day O'Connor
D. Rosa Parks

10. Which one of these was not one of the 13 original colonies?

A. Georgia
B. New Hampshire
C. Maine
D. Rhode Island

ECONOMICS

11. Water, plants, and minerals are things that come from nature and examples of what kind of resources?

A. scarce resources
B. capital resources
C. human resources
D. natural resources

12. A _____ is someone who uses a good or a service.

A. consumer
B. producer
C. worker
D. resident

13. A _____ is someone who makes something (a good) or provides a service.

A. boss
B. consumer
C. resident
D. producer

14. Which one of these is an example of a basic need?

A. video game
B. shelter
C. toy
D. microwave

15. Which one of these is an example of a "want"?

A. food
B. water
C. clothing
D. tablet

GEOGRAPHY

Use the map above to answer questions 16 to 23.

16. The capital of the United States is ___.

A. Washington State
B. New York City
C. Los Angeles
D. Washington, D.C.

17. Find letter G on the map. What state is this?

A. New York
B. California
C. Nevada
D. Oregon

18. Find letter H on the map. What state is this?

A. Texas
B. New Mexico
C. Arizona
D. Oklahoma

19. Find letter K on the map. What state is this?

A. California
B. Alabama
C. Florida
D. Georgia

20. The state in letter K forms what kind of body of land?

A. gulf
B. island
C. peninsula
D. valley

21. For this question you will also use the state with letter K.
Find the compass. What body of water lies to the east of the state with letter K?

A. Pacific Ocean
B. Atlantic Ocean
C. Gulf of Mexico
D. Mississippi River

22. What country is to the north of the United States?

A. Canada
B. Mexico
C. Alaska
D. North Dakota

23. Find the state with the letter G again. What body of water lies to the west of this state?

A. Colorado River
B. Lake Tahoe
C. Atlantic Ocean
D. Pacific Ocean

ECONOMICS

24. Kelly goes to the toy store. She buys a beach ball. A beach ball is an example of a _____.

A. service
B. product
C. food
D. need

25. A hairstylist is a type of job. A hairstylist provides _____.

A. a consumer
B. a natural resource
C. a service
D. a need

26. When you trade goods and services without exchanging money, this is called __.

A. bartering
B. credit
C. cash
D. economy

27. When people depend on each other for goods and services, this is called ___.

A. bartering
B. producers
C. economics
D. interdependence

28. A printing business buys a new printing press. This printing press is an example of a ____.

A. limited resource
B. natural resource
C. capital resource
D. consumer

This is the end of this section and the practice test.

Word Analysis Question Text (for p.66-69)

- **Cut out this page.**
- **You must read these questions to your child.**

Example Questions on p.66
Example 1. Pick the word that begins with the sound: "sh".
Example 2. How many syllables does this word have: "sofa"?
Example 3. What is the prefix in this word: "unafraid"?

Questions beginning on p.67
1. Pick the word that begins with the same sound as this word: "tiger".
2. Pick the word that begins with the sound: "ch".
3. Pick the word that begins with the sound: "th".
4. Pick the word that rhymes with the word "flight."
5. If you replace the middle sound of the word "fin" with the "short a" sound, which word do you get?
6. Pick the ending sounds of this word: "raft".
7. Pick the word that ends with this sound: "sh"
8. Pick the middle sound of this word: "back".
9. What is the first syllable of this word: reflect?
10. Pick the word that starts with a closed syllable.
11. How many syllables does this word have: "limit"?
12. How many syllables does this word have: "detective"?
13. Pick the word that has a silent letter: mask, teen, wink, muscle
14. Pick the word that has a silent letter: seem, tusk, sail, sign
15. Pick the word that has a silent letter: thumb, glitter, insect, follow
16. Pick the word that has a silent letter: hippo, sword, monkey, flash
17. What is the suffix in this word: "hopeful"?
18. What does this word mean: "kindness" ?
19. If you took away the first syllable of the word "independent", what would be the first syllable?
20. What is the last syllable of this word: "thickness"?
21. What is the last syllable of this word: "shovel"?
22. What is the last syllable of this word: "bottle"?
23. What is the last syllable of this word: "television"?
24. Which word is a compound word?
25. Which word is a compound word?
26. Which words create the compound word "anybody"?
27. Which word means "a person who writes"?
28. Look at the 4 pictures. Which one shows a word that has a "long a" sound?
29. Look at the 4 pictures. Which picture begins with the same sound as this word: "winter"?
30. Look at the 4 pictures. Which one shows a word that has a "long i" sound?
31. Look at the 4 pictures. Which picture begins with the same sound as this word: "bubble"?
32. Look at the 4 pictures. Which picture begins with the same sound as this word: "harp"?
33. Look at the 4 pictures. Which picture begins with the same sound as this word: "cereal"?

Listening Question Text (for p.70-75)

- **Cut out this page.**
- **You must read these questions to your child.**

<u>Example Questions on p.70</u>
-Example 1: Samantha wanted to bake cookies for her family. She gathered all the ingredients, but when she started mixing them, she realized that she had forgotten to buy eggs. She quickly ran to the store to purchase them. After she came back, Samantha finished making the dough and baked the cookies. Her family loved them!
Question: In the story, you heard the word "purchase." Which word is closest in meaning to "purchase?"

-Example 2: *Which picture shows two black circles to the right of 1 gray circle?*

<u>Questions beginning on p.71</u>
1. Maya's house is on the edge of a forest. Whenever the wind blows strongly, leaves and branches end up scattered across her yard. Next weekend, Maya and her family are planning to have a picnic in the backyard.
-*Question: What will happen if the wind blows strongly during the picnic?*

2. Luke was getting ready for his piano recital. He practiced every day for a week. On Monday, he played for his dad, who said he sounded great. On Wednesday, he went to the concert hall to practice with his piano teacher, and everything went well. The next day, he finally played in front of an audience, and everyone clapped for him.
-*Question: When did Luke play in front of an audience?*

3. Ethan was washing dishes after dinner. As he reached for the next plate to wash, he accidentally dropped it, spilling some of the leftover food onto the floor. Ethan noticed his dog, Max, running from the hall into the kitchen, wagging his tail excitedly.
-*Question: What probably happened next?*

4. David is focused on staying healthy. He only has food and drinks that are good for him. In the morning he either has orange juice or a smoothie to drink. At lunch, for a drink, he has milk. In the evening, he drinks water. This morning, when he went to the fridge to get something to drink, he saw that they were out of orange juice. After breakfast, David went for a jog around the neighborhood. In the afternoon, he went to meet his friends.
-*Question: What did David drink this morning?*

5. Maria was excited to visit the zoo with her family. When they arrived, she saw so many different animals. The elephants were her favorite because they were so big and playful. However, as they approached the lion's cage, they noticed it was empty. The zookeeper explained that the lion was resting inside its den, away from the visitors.
-*Question: In the story, you heard the word "approached." Which word is closest in meaning to "approached"?*

6. In recent years, coral reefs around the world have been dying due to pollution and warming ocean water. The reefs are home to many types of sea life. Scientists are trying to find ways to prevent this, but there are no easy solutions.
-*Question: The story uses the word "solutions." In the story, what does the word "solutions" mean?*

7. Ben and Lisa went on a field trip to the science museum. When they arrived, the students were split into groups. One group went to the dinosaur exhibit, while the other group went to the solar system exhibit first. Ben visited the dinosaur exhibit first, but Lisa visited the solar system exhibit first. After the exhibits, the whole class had lunch together in the museum's cafeteria. Before leaving, they stopped by the gift shop.
-*Question: Which one did Lisa most likely see first?*

8. Maya decided to help her parents by doing some chores in the yard. First, she picked up all the fallen branches from the ground. Then, she raked the leaves into a pile and put them into bags. After that, she watered the flowers in the garden. Finally, she swept the porch to clear away the dirt and leaves.
-*Question: Which chore did Maya not do?*

9. Jay participated in his school's spelling bee competition. To reach the final round, he had to correctly spell at least seven words out of ten. Jay studied for weeks, practicing with his parents every evening. His classmates cheered him on during the event. After the competition, Jay and his family went out for ice cream to celebrate his hard work.
-*Question: How many words did Jay probably spell correctly?*

10. Liam was hiking on a trail in a national park when he spotted something unusual. A large tree had fallen across the path, blocking the way for other hikers. The tree was too big for Liam to move on his own. He didn't want anyone to get hurt trying to climb over it, so Liam took out his phone to call someone who would be able to help.
-*Question: Who did Liam probably call?*

11. Emily and her dad went to the garden center to buy flowers for their backyard. They walked around looking at all the different types of plants. After picking out some colorful flowers, they took them to the cashier and paid. Then, they loaded the flowers into their car and drove home to plant them in the garden.
-*Question: What did Emily and her dad do right before they loaded the flowers into the car?*

12. Kelly has a tennis lesson for one hour every Saturday morning. The lesson starts at 9:30 AM. Her mom usually wakes her up at 8:30 AM so she has time to get dressed and eat breakfast. Today, though, her mom forgot to set an alarm, and Kelly woke up at 9:20 AM. She still needs to put on her tennis outfit, eat breakfast, and grab her racket before leaving.
-*Question: What will probably happen next?*

13. Emily went to the aquarium with her older brother. They saw a shark, dolphin, sea turtle, and jellyfish. After exploring the exhibits, they stopped at the gift shop. After they bought a souvenir, they went to the grocery store.
-*Question: Which answer shows an animal Emily and her brother did not see at the aquarium?*

14. Sarah and her friends, Emma and Carl, love to bake together. Sarah bakes cupcakes, Emma makes cookies, and Carl specializes in donuts. They decided to start a small bakery, but they realized they also needed someone who could bake bread and cakes. They are currently looking for someone to help with those items.
-Question: Mark the answer that shows what Sarah bakes.

15. Jake and his friends were painting pictures of dogs. Jake chose to paint his dog black, while his friend Noah painted his dog white. Their friend Ava painted her dog gray. After they finished, they decided to paint a picture of a dog together, but they hadn't decided what color the dog would be.
-Question: Which color did Jake use to paint his dog?

16. David and his friends were baking pies for a school event. They made several types of pies: a blueberry pie, apple pie, strawberry pie, and pumpkin pie. After they finished baking, they each had a slice of their favorite pie. Once they cleaned up the kitchen, they went outside to play soccer.
-Question: Mark the answer that shows the food that David and his friends did not use to bake their pies.

17. Which picture shows a girl facing left and a boy facing right?

18. Jessica and her friends planned a surprise party for their friend, Rachel. Jessica brought a teddy bear and a basketball as gifts for Rachel. Another friend, Jake, brought a bike and a doll that Rachel had been wanting for a while. When Rachel arrived at the party, she was excited to see all her friends and the thoughtful gifts they had for her.
-Question: Which answer shows an item Jessica brought to the party?

19. Maria has a pet fish. Kevin has a cat. Ella has a dog.
Which picture shows Kevin's pet on the right, Ella's pet in the middle and Maria's pet on the left?

20. Alex was sitting on the dock by the lake with his fishing pole. Alex and his dad arrived early in the morning to fish, and the sun was starting to rise. Alex's friends jumped into the lake and invited him to join them. He decided to finish fishing first, but he went back to his house to change before joining them in the water.
-Question: What did Alex probably put on?

21. Which answer choice shows this: the word "tree" to the right of the word "flower" and the word "bee" to the right of the word "ant"?

22. Lee bought a cookie. Rex bought a cupcake. Sandra bought ice cream.
-Question: Which choice shows this: Lee's dessert on the left, Sandra's dessert in the middle, and Rex's dessert on the right.

23. Fran has 3 dice. She rolls them and here are the 3 numbers she gets: 2, 4, 6.
-Question: Which picture shows the numbers that Fran rolled?

24. Your little brother went to the toy store to pick out some new toys. He bought a toy train, toy car, toy helicopter, and drum. After he finished shopping, he met his friend at the park to play. Later, he returned home and put all his new toys in his room.
-Question: Which answer shows a toy that he did not buy at the toy store?

25. Rita enjoys making jewelry in her free time. For her next project, she decided to create four different bracelets using beads of different colors: white, gray, black, and blue stripes. So far, she has already made bracelets with white, gray, and blue striped beads. Rita is excited to finish her last bracelet this weekend.
-Question: Which answer choice shows the color of the bracelet Rita has not yet made?

26. Ben and his mom planted a flower garden in their backyard. They used a shovel, watering can, and garden gloves. After they finished planting, Ben invited his neighbors to come see the new garden. They spent the afternoon admiring the flowers and the rest of the garden.
-Question: Which answer shows a gardening tool that Ben and his mother used?

27. Which answer choice shows this: a fish to the left of an octopus and a dolphin to the left of a turtle?

Answer Key

Reading

Reading Passage 1:
1. C. see 2nd sentence
2. B. The passage states that male lions are responsible for protecting the pride from threats.
3. A. According to the passage, they are usually active in the early morning or evening when it's cooler.
4. B. The passage mentions that habitat loss and illegal hunting are major threats to their survival.

Reading Passage 2:
1. C. They use their communication system to work together to hunt for food and protect each other from predators.
2. C. see 2nd sentence
3. D. They are often seen jumping out of the water, riding waves, and interacting with humans, which shows their playful nature.
4. B. Pollution, fishing nets, and habitat loss are some of the man-made dangers they face in the wild.

Reading Passage 3:
1. C. The poem compares life without dreams to a "broken-winged bird that cannot fly," suggesting that life will feel hopeless.
2. A. The speaker describes life without dreams as a "barren field frozen with snow," emphasizing how sad it can become.
3. B. This means to hold onto them tightly and not let go.
4. D. These emphasize the sadness and emptiness that comes with losing dreams, showing the importance of holding on to them.

Reading Passage 4:
1. A. The passage mentions that Thomas dreamed of becoming a great baker, which is why he visited the bakery every day to watch the baker work.
2. D. The baker invited Thomas inside and let him help, which is how Thomas learned to bake.
3. B. The baker fell ill, which is why Thomas was asked to bake the bread.
4. B. The villagers exclaimed that Thomas's bread was the best they had ever tasted.
5. A. The passage suggests that Thomas realized his dream of becoming a great baker was possible with practice and patience.

Reading Passage 5:
1. B.   2. C. see 3rd sentence   3. A.
4. D. They migrate to follow the summer season.   5. B. They have the longest migration in the world.

Reading Passage 6:
1. B. Sarah had always wanted to explore the Amazon rainforest, which suggests that she wanted to visit a place she had never been.
2. C. Sarah joined a tour group and hiked through the rainforest.
3. D. The guide explained that it produces much of the world's oxygen and is home to many species.
4. C. Sarah learned about the dangers it faces, including deforestation and climate change.
5. A. Sarah returned home determined to help protect the environment and raise awareness about rainforest conservation.

Reading Passage 7:

1. B. Maria's favorite section was the mystery novels.
2. A. Maria explained to Mrs. Patel that she was entering a reading challenge at school and needed to read 10 books in a month, which is why she checked out more books than usual.
3. C. Mrs. Patel handed Maria a bookmark with tips on how to keep track of the books she read.
4. D. Maria was excited to start her reading challenge after leaving the library.
5. C. Maria always tried to solve the mystery before the characters did.

Reading Passage 8:

1. D. The passage mentions that Jack and his grandfather went fishing at the lake every Saturday.
2. B. Jack shouted excitedly because his line tugged hard, and he caught a large fish.
3. C. After helping Jack reel in the fish, his grandfather complimented him by saying this.
4. A. See the last sentence in the passage.
5. A. Jack loved the quiet mornings, listening to the birds, and watching the sunrise.

Written Expression

1. A. "Goes" should be "go."
2. A. "Has" should be "have."   3. C. The plural of "foot" is "feet," not "foots."
4. C. "Ate" should be "eat."
5. B. "Her and her sister" should be "she and her sister."
6. D.   7. D.
8. C. "There" should be "their."
9. A. The placement of "nearly" is incorrect. The word "nearly" (called a "modifier") should be after the subject "Emma." It could also be rewritten as "Emma ate nearly all her sandwich."
10. C. "Your" should be "you're" (as in "you are").
11. C. "Makes" should be "make."   12. D.
13. B. The correct past tense of the verb "break" is not "breaked," it is "broke."
14. C. "Them" should be "the."
15. B. The sentence needs a plural noun ("boxes") and not a possessive noun ("box's").
16. B. This sentence best introduces the main idea of the passage.
17. A. (This is correct because it means the planets orbit the sun, which is scientifically correct.)
18. C. This talks about playing soccer, which is unrelated to the main focus of the trip.
19. D.   20. D.   21. A. It combines the two sentences clearly and uses correct punctuation.
22. C. This sentence talks about what the narrator did at camp last summer.
23. A. It sums up the excitement and positive feeling of the passage.
24. B. It is in the correct tense (past tense) and keeps the sentence from being too long.
25. D. Sentence 8 should have gone after Sentence 3.
26. A. While this sentence is an interesting fact, it does not belong in the passage.
27. C. It wraps up the passage and sums up the event.
28. D.   29. C. It is written in the past tense, like the rest of the paragraph.
30. D. is correct because the narrator's dad's Halloween costume does not have to do with the paragraph, even though the costume was George Washington.
31. A. It concludes the paragraph well by summing up the narrator's enthusiasm for future trips.
32. C. This choice uses commas correctly.
33. C. The ice cream outing is not directly related to the main theme.
34. B. This is the best way to combine the sentences and does not create a run-on sentence.
35. A. This wraps up the passage. The others are not directly related to the passage in a way that provides a good conclusion.

Mathematics

1. C   2. B   3. C   4. B   5. D   6. B   7. C   8. D

9. A: John started reading at 2:30 p.m. and read for 1.5 hours, which makes 4:00 p.m. His sister called 15 minutes before he finished reading, so that would be 3:45 p.m.

10. D

11. C: Starting at 14 and skip counting by 7s gives the sequence: 14, 21, 28, 35, 42. This shows that the rule of skipping by 7s fits the pattern.

12. A: The fractions have the same numerator. Because they do, you must look at the denominators in order to compare the fractions. If fractions have the same numerator, that means that the higher the denominator, the smaller the fraction will be.

13. A

14. B: On Tuesday, she collects 8 seashells. Then, each day, she collects 5 seashells. So, over three days (Wednesday, Thursday, and Friday), that will be $3 \times 5 = 15$ seashells. So, she will have $8 + 15 = 23$ seashells by the end of Friday.

15. C: $45 \div (10 \div 2) = 9$; $45 \div 5 = 9$

16. C: We have: $(5 \times 8) \times 3 + 5$; $5 \times 8 = 40$, then $40 \times 3 = 120$, and finally $120 + 5 = 125$. Option C, $(8 \times 3) \times 5 + 5$, simplifies in the same way: $8 \times 3 = 24$, then $24 \times 5 = 120$, finally $120 + 5 = 125$.

17. D   18. D   19. B   20. A: 15.7 - 11.4 = 4.3.

21. C: $154 \times 4 = 616$, which is between 600 and 700

22. B: To find the amount of water Mel added, subtract the amount already in the fishbowl (8 cups) from the total capacity (15 cups). This gives us 15 - 8 = 7 cups.

23. A   24. C   25. D   26. B   27. A   28. B   29. C

30. B   31. D

32. C: a polygon is a flat, closed shape made up of straight line segments connected end-to-end; a pentagon has 5 sides

33. D: $1.10 is less than $1.25   34. D   35. A

36. B: +6 in between each number

37. D: a line of symmetry is an imaginary line that cuts a shape perfectly in half

38. C: this shape has 4 sides

39. A: add the 3 known sides: 29+12+11=52; then subtract, 80-52 = 28

40. A

41. B: there are more sun stickers, so she is more likely to pick a sun sticker

42. A: add the number of pets (24), then divide by the number of kids (8) (The mean is the same as the average.)

43. B: the mode is the most common number in the group

44. B: To find the range, subtract the smallest and largest number: 5 - 1 = 4

45. C: $700-$500 = $200   46. D: $100 + $500 + $400 = $1,000

47. A: $100 + $500 + $700 + $400 + $300 + $200 = $2,200

48. B: 80 + 10 = 90 degrees

49. C: You must count the shape's line segments and the lines inside the shape

50. D: This shape does not have a corner that looks like the letter "L" - where two lines meet perfectly perpendicular to each other.

Vocabulary

1. B. absorb = to soak up or to take in   2. D. approach = to move toward
3. C. consider = to think about   4. A. contain = to hold or to have within it
5. C. delicate = easily broken/damaged   6. B. ancient = very old
7. D. decay = to slowly break down or rot

Vocabulary, continued

8. A. rely = to depend on someone or something for help or support
9. B. swift = quick
10. D. digest = to break down; here, to break down food so your body can use it for energy
11. A. recall = remember   12. C. frail = weak and easily broken
13. B. gradual = slow/ happening slowly over time
14. D. intend = to plan to / to have in mind as a purpose to do something
15. C. primary = main / something that is the most important (it can also mean "first")
16. B. solution = answer   17. D. theory = an idea used to explain something
18. A. triumph = to win   19. A. fortunate = lucky   20. B. distant = far off / not near
21. D. brief = short   22. C. examine = look carefully at   23. A. imitate = copy
24. C. locate = to find / to find the position of something   25. B. mystifying = confusing
26. D. confess = to tell / make something known   27. C. typical = normal, regular
28. A. occur = happen   29. D. diagram = a drawing that shows the parts of something
30. B. irritate = to annoy / to bother

Spelling

1. D. books   2. C. always   3. C. such   4. D. both   5. B. added   6. A. libraries   7. D. mean
8. B. guess   9. C. jury   10. E.   11. D. forty   12. B. dollar   13. D. funniest 14. B. favorite
15. E.   16. A. sickness   17. A. double   18. E.   19. B. calmly   20. D. whistle
21. C. quick   22. E.   23. B. bottom   24. B. soak

Capitalization

1. A. Saturday   2. B. Chicago   3. B. Lincoln   4. A. mountains (should not be capitalized)
5. D.   6. A. North (North America is a continent)   7. B. Memorial Day
8. A. Brownies, cookies, and cakes (cookies and cakes should not be capitalized)   9. D.
10. C. France   11. B. As   12. B. Max   13. D.   14. D.
15. A. explorer (should not be capitalized)   16. C. Hidden Treasures
17. B. U.S.   18. A. *The Wizard of Oz*   19. C. Kerry's   20. C. yours (should not be capitalized)

Punctuation

1. B: There should be a comma after "math" to separate the items in the list properly.
2. C: There should be a comma after "22." When a date consists of the day of the month followed by the year, there should be a comma right after the day of the month.
3. B: There should be a comma after the word "No." When words like "No" start a sentence, they should be followed by a comma.
4. A: There should not be a comma after "Polar bears."
5. C: There should be commas between the activities in the list ("piano, writing songs, and performing").
6. D   7. C: There should be an apostrophe in "can't" because it's a contraction.
8. D   9. C: There should be a period after "Mr." to correctly abbreviate the title.
10. C: There should be commas between the countries in the list ("Egypt, Greece, and China").
11. C: A period is needed instead of a question mark after "sure," as it is a statement, not a question.
12. A: There shouldn't be a period after the word "landmarks." The word "in" following the period is not capitalized, indicating that the sentence is incorrectly divided.
13. C: There should be a period after "Dr." (Dr. Smith) as it is an abbreviation of doctor.
14. B: The comma is in the wrong place. It should be: on December 31, 2010

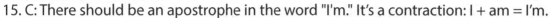

Punctuation, continued

15. C: There should be an apostrophe in the word "I'm." It's a contraction: I + am = I'm.

16. B: There should be a period after the word "square," as this word ends a sentence. A new sentence begins with "Sarah."

17. A: There should be a question mark after the word "that" instead of a comma. The word "Can" at the beginning of the sentence tells us that it's a question.

18. D

19. B: No period is needed after the word "late." The word "to" following the period is not capitalized.

20. B: There should be a period before the word "She." The word "She" is capitalized, showing us that it starts a new sentence and needs a period before it.

Computation

1. A 2. C 3. A 4. D 5. A 6. B 7. A 8. C 9. A 10. D 11. C 12. A 13. D
14. D 15. A 16. B 17. B 18. A 19. D 20. A 21. B 22. B 23. D 24. A 25. B 26. C

Word Analysis

1. C 2. A 3. D 4. B 5. B 6. A 7. C 8. D 9. A 10. B 11. B 12. C 13. D
14. D 15. A 16. B 17. B 18. C 19. C 20. B 21. C 22. B 23. C 24. D 25. C 26. A
27. C 28. B 29. A 30. B 31. A 32. D 33. C

Listening

1. C 2. C 3. A 4. C 5. D 6. A 7. B 8. D 9. D 10. B 11. C 12. D 13. A 14. C
15. A 16. B 17. D 18. A 19. B 20. C 21. D 22. B 23. B 24. A 25. D 26. C 27. A

Science

1. A 2. C 3. A 4. B 5. C 6. D 7. D 8. A 9. B 10. C 11. C 12. A 13. D
14. C 15. B 16. A 17. C 18. C 19. B 20. A 21. B 22. A 23. C 24. A 25. D

Social Studies

1. B 2. C 3. A 4. C 5. D 6. D 7. A 8. B 9. B 10. C 11. D 12. A 13. D 14. B
15. D 16. D 17. B 18. A 19. C 20. C 21. B 22. A 23. D 24. B 25. C 26. A 27. D 28. C

Made in United States
Cleveland, OH
08 April 2025

15886310R00057